Building the Hoover Dam

AF580823

by John Manos

Scott Foresman
is an imprint of

Glenview, Illinois • Boston, Massachusetts • Mesa, Arizona
Shoreview, Minnesota • Upper Saddle River, New Jersey

Photographs
Every effort has been made to secure permission and provide appropriate credit for photographic material. The publisher deeply regrets any omission and pledges to correct errors called to its attention in subsequent editions.

Unless otherwise acknowledged, all photographs are the property of Pearson Education, Inc.

Photo locators denoted as follows: Top (T), Center (C), Bottom (B), Left (L), Right (R), Background (Bkgd).

Cover: ©Patrick Eden/Alamy Images; 4 ©Lester Lefkowitz/Corbis; 5 (BL) ©Jupiter Images/Brand X/Alamy, (BCL) ©Jupiter Images/Goodshoot/Alamy, (BC) ©Flip Chalfant/ Getty Images, (BR) ©Lester Lefkowitz/Corbis; 7 ©Bettmann/Corbis; 8 AP Images; 9 ©Underwood & Underwood/Corbis; 10 (BL) The Image Works, Inc., (BCL, BC, BR) AP Images; 11 ©Bettmann/Corbis; 12 ©Lester Lefkowitz/Corbis; 13 ©James Marshall/Corbis

ISBN 13: 978-0-328- 39370-1
ISBN 10: 0-328- 39370-3

1 2 3 4 5 6 7 8 9 10 V010 17 16 15 14 13 12 11 10 09 08

TABLE OF CONTENTS

Chapter 1

The Hoover Dam

The Hoover **Dam** stands like a huge wall on the Colorado River between the states of Nevada and Arizona. A dam is a huge wall built to control the flow of water on a river. It blocks water behind it. Workers on a dam can control how much water gets through the dam.

The Hoover Dam.

If you ever visit the Hoover Dam, you'll be surprised by its size. It's one of the biggest dams ever built. The dam is made mostly of **concrete**. There is enough concrete in the Hoover Dam to make a sidewalk that could wrap around Earth. The base of the dam is so thick that two football fields could fit next to each other inside it!

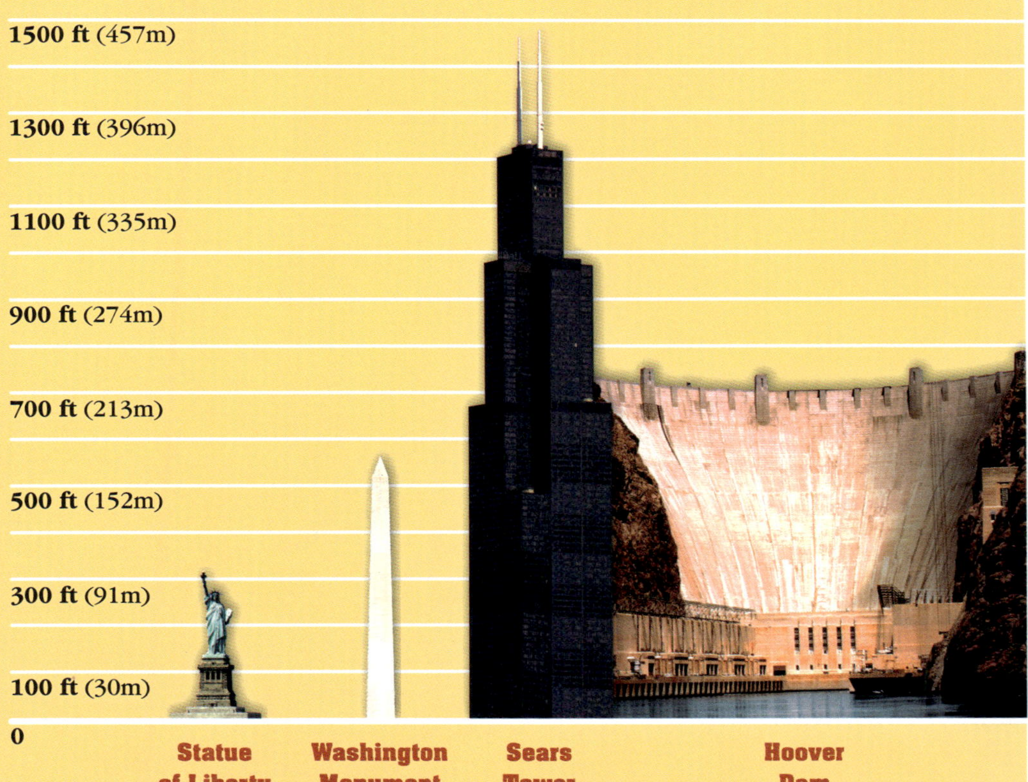

Chapter 2
Why the Hoover Dam Was Built

The Hoover Dam blocks the flow of the Colorado River. Before the dam was built, too much rain sometimes made the Colorado River overflow and flood the land. The flooding was **significant** enough to hurt farms. The soil became too wet for crops to grow.

At other times, there wasn't enough rain for crops to grow. Farmers weren't sure how much water they could use without running out. They didn't have control over the level of water in the area.

Many people **identified** these as big problems. The Hoover Dam was built to solve these problems.

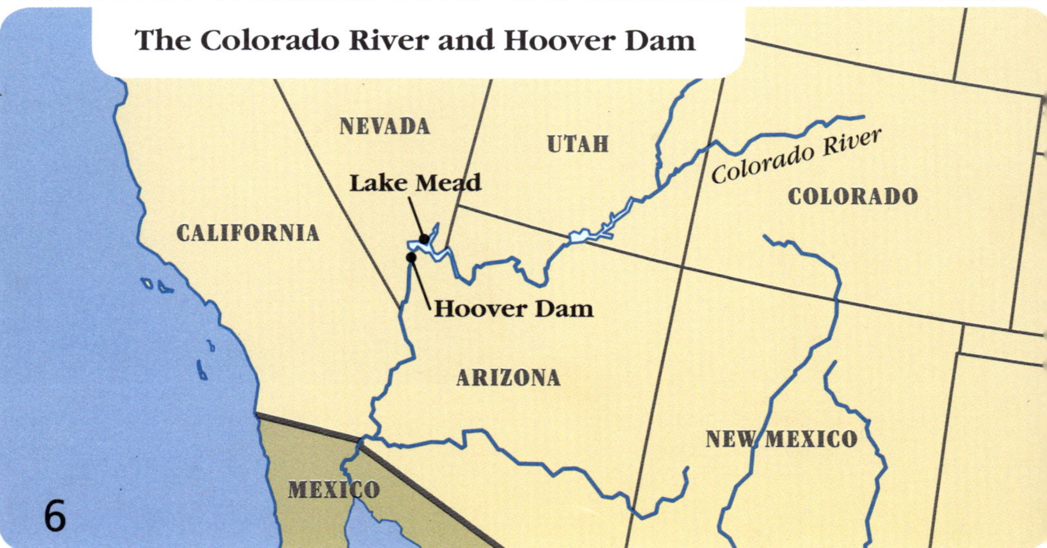

Chapter 3
Building the Dam

Work began on the Hoover Dam in 1931. At that time, many people in the country didn't have jobs. People heard there might be jobs building the dam. Many people traveled from all over to work on the dam.

At first, Hoover Dam workers and their families lived in camps. The people had no water or electricity. But they were happy to have a job. Then a new town called Boulder City was built for the workers. Boulder City had houses with water and electric lights.

Boulder City

Building the dam was hard work. It couldn't be built just anywhere along the Colorado River. It had to be built in a small **canyon**. A canyon is a narrow valley with high, steep sides. The land around the dam needed to be strong.

A lot of work had to be done before the dam could be built. First, people moved rocks from the canyon. They hung on long ropes to take loose rocks away. It was very dangerous work.

The workers had to get used to very hot weather. Some people from other parts of the country never got used to it. "I'm sick from the heat," said one of the workers. "I have to leave the canyon."

People worked 500 feet above the river.

The river was also in the way. In order for the dam to be built, the flow of the river needed to change. Four big tunnels were dug next to the river. The water from the river could flow through the tunnels.

Then rocks and dirt were dumped into the river in two places to make smaller dams. This made the river flow into the tunnels and away from the new dam. If workers hadn't done this, the river might have backed up and flooded the land.

A tunnel during construction

It was time for the concrete to be poured. The dam rose taller and taller in the canyon. After much work, the dam was finally finished.

The tunnels were closed, and the river began to flow to the new dam. The water filled in to form a very big lake. It was named Lake Mead.

More than 5,000 workers **participated** in building the Hoover Dam. They worked hard for almost five years. The Hoover Dam changed the area, and the workers had helped. Many of them chose to live nearby with their families. People still live in Boulder City today.

The Hoover Dam was completed in about five years.

Chapter 4
The Hoover Dam and Lake Mead Today

The Hoover Dam still controls the flow of the Colorado River. Lake Mead holds so much water that farmers are no longer afraid that there won't be enough water for their crops.

At one time people worried that the water in Lake Mead would get too high. They worried that water might go over the top of the Hoover Dam. The dam wouldn't last long if that happened. To fix this problem, special places were built where the extra water could flow. So far, there hasn't been a problem with flooding.

Hoover Dam helped stop floods on the Colorado River.

Lake Mead is a source of drinking water and water for people's homes too. Millions of people get their water from Lake Mead.

The water in Lake Mead is also used to produce electricity. Special pipes carry water into machines that use it to produce electricity. These machines can produce enough electricity for more than one million people!

These machines produce electricity.

Lake Mead is the largest man-made lake in the United States. Many people boat and fish on Lake Mead.

People from all over the world will visit the Hoover Dam this year. They'll take tours of the dam. They may even drive across the highway that goes across the top of the dam!

You can drive across the Hoover Dam!

Now Try This

Building a Model Dam

You and friends can have fun and learn more about dams by making a model of a river and a dam. You'll need a pan that can hold water. You'll also need enough sand to cover the bottom of the pan. A small jar of water is the only other thing you'll need.

You'll have fun watching a lake form!